Pluviophile

By Raquel Z. Duarte

Copyright © 2017 Raquel Z. Duarte

All rights reserved.

ISBN-13: 978-0999592328
ISBN-10: 0999592327

Dedicated to the one who taught me how to read and write.

My queen.

I love you, Mama.

[Gratitude]

. . .

Before you begin to explore these pages, thanks needs to be made to certain individuals without whom this collection never would have been started. This is my section to honor and praise the impact they had on helping make this book become a reality.

First and foremost, my Jesus. He gave me this love for writing, and the talent to express my thoughts through the written word. Without Him, none of this would be.

My Mama - my biggest encourager, my biggest fan, the one who always pushed me to write, write, write. I honor you.

My Russian Grandpa - from whom I acquired my love of writing and reading, and who has the best handwriting ever.

My Peruvian Grandpa - who always encouraged me to pursue what I was passionate about.

Jade Fletcher, Mitchell Glockling, and Brittany Pannapacker - supporters through this whole process.

To certain individuals who inspired many of the writings in this collection, you know who you are. Or you will know, anyway, when you read what I've written about you.

To family, friends, blog/Instagram followers - who have kept coming back to read more and continued to ask me when I would publish a book.
Well, here it is.

[Salutations]

. . .

I have always been one to believe that if a writer's work isn't affecting the reader some way, somehow then their writing is not real.

Maybe the words don't form eloquently.
Maybe what they write about is something from another realm.
Maybe it's not supposed to make sense.

And that's okay.

    Actually, it's perfect.

Because, you see, when it comes to writing "correctly", there's no right or wrong.

You write what you want to write.

"Flow" and "natural" have nothing to do with it. No one has authority to say if it's good or bad.
And if the reader finishes reading your words and asks, "What in the world did I just read?", then you have succeeded.
If they say, "This was beautiful" or "This was sad". Well done.
For in all these instances, it was real.

You have made them *feel* something.

And as a writer, that is - and always will be - the greatest goal.
The greatest accomplishment.
The greatest reward.

And that is what I wish for you through these pages, through the words I have painstakingly, heartfully written.

I hope they're relatable.
    I hope they touch you.
        I hope you feel them.

Pluviophile (noun)

```
A lover of rain; someone who finds
joy and peace of mind during rainy
                days
```

I. Tempest

"We will carry pieces of all those who have built and broken us."
- Atticus

Him Vs. Me

. . .

He wanted coffee
        I was tea.

He wanted money
        I was poetry.

He wanted sunshine
        I was made of rain.

He wanted arm candy
        But I wasn't a prom queen.

He liked to get drunk on weekends
        I wanted my sober best friend.

He said he wanted a family
        I told him I wanted a ring.

He said "I love you"
        And I believed him.

But now it's just me.

I Taught You What Love Is

. . .

One of the deepest and most agonizing questions someone could ask themselves is: **"Why was I not good enough?"**

When I did all I could do, when I said all I could say, when I loved with all I had in me...but in the end, it must not have been enough.

I wasn't enough.

Or so you thought, it seemed.

See, the thing about being vulnerable and loving someone and investing in their life is that you are giving them every open door to hurting you. Like Augustus said in The Fault In Our Stars - "You don't get to choose if you get hurt in this world. But you do have a say in who hurts you."

Loving someone and trusting them to not rip my heart out from the seams is an act of faith that takes all the courage in the world to muster.

But when it all crashed down around me, in a myriad of shooting stars that dispersed, one of the first questions that will come to mind was simply one word:

"Why?"

It can be asked in many different forms. A cry, a scream, a gut-wrenching sob, or merely a whisper.
I think I may have asked it in all of those ways.

And over time, I've missed you. I've missed how you loved me, how you made me feel, the things we used to do together, the connection that we had. But what you may not know is that I've realized something.

It took many sleepless nights, long, arduous thought processes, furrowed brows, and quiet tears to unravel all the knots of confusion and pain.

And I finally realized that: how you loved me was so much of a reflection of everything I was, everything I gave to you, and everything I am.

Looking back now, I must've been so blind because I see now that it was I who taught you. I taught you how to feel again. I was the example you needed in your life to make you see and understand that there *is* such a thing as unconditional love, and there *is* such a thing as faithfulness, and there *is* such a thing as a woman who wants to be with you and only you.
And that woman was me.

I wondered "Why?" for so long after, but now I no longer ask that. Because I know I was enough.
In fact, I was too much.
It scared you.
I scared you.
The strength, peace, love and beauty I felt when I was with you, I thought it was because of you.
But it wasn't.
I thought I enamored you and loved you in ways you never knew existed because you couldn't take your eyes off of me. I made you feel alive again. I taught you what love is. But you didn't know how to accept it. And then I thought I was the problem. I thought I wasn't enough.

But I know now that I already was these things.

Long before I met you.

And I continued to be all of this, even after you left.

Because the person I am when I'm around you isn't *because* of you. It's because of my love for you. And even if you aren't around to see it, I'm still strong, and beautiful, and full of love. And I always will be.

I started writing this for my audience, in an attempt to encourage the recent heartbreaks that I know of, but not even halfway through, I realized that I was writing this for myself.

About myself.

And the tears were freeing.

Some Of the Things I Want To Tell You

. . .

I want to tell you that the first time I saw you, not only did my heart go wild, but my brain did too.

I want to tell you that I remembered the drink you ordered but I asked you to repeat it just so I could hear your voice again.

I want to tell you that I wished there hadn't been other customers in line behind you because I wanted you to stay as long as possible.

I want to tell you that your eyes captured me. And I've never met anyone else with the same color as yours are.

I want to tell you that it took everything in me to not let the flush rise to my cheeks when our eyes found each other.

I want to tell you that every moment I spent with you after our first meeting was like a perfect scene in a storybook.

I want to tell you that I believe you loved me, but that's what scared you the most.

I want to tell you that I don't hate you for the way you hurt me.

I want to tell you that so many little things remind me of you and bring you to memory.

    I want to tell you that I wrote this poem about you, for you.

I want to tell you that there are countless times in my day that I pick up my phone to call you, but then remember that you were the one who deleted me from your life.

    And that's okay, I guess.

Because not everyone is meant to stick around forever. And I guess that's true for you and me and our story.

I also want to tell you that I know we were meant to be together. Maybe not for the rest of our lives.

    But baby, for a time, I'm so glad I could call you mine.

And I titled this only *some of the things I want to tell you* because if you want to know the rest, maybe that will be enough to make you come back someday.

Ashes Among Your Cigarettes

. . .

When I met you, not only did fireworks display brilliant colors in my brain, but so did sirens, alarms, warnings to not let myself get attached to you.
They told me not to get too close or I would get burnt.

But I didn't listen.

And I learned the hard way, I guess.

I learned that not all good things are meant to stay.

And if something seems too good to be true, then it most likely is.

I shouldn't have fallen for you.

But it's as if I couldn't help myself.

It was almost like I had gone sky-diving.
Once you jump out of the plane, there's no going back. There's only falling.
      And maybe regret.

And maybe this is why I never want to go sky-diving

Because it reminds me of you.

The initial fear, the thrill, the adrenaline rush, seeing the ground get closer and closer as you fall,

                                          fall,

                                                              fall.

And that sting of regret.

It comes every once in a while

Shooting through my veins

Sending signals to my brain, reminding me of all the times I thought you'd stay.

You're my biggest regret.
But damn, is it really a regret if I would do it all over again?

Just don't come back.

Please.

Because I want you.

And if I think I'm broken now, then I know I'd burn to ashes if I ever let you back in.

And I'm not sure what you'd do with my remains,
But I would hope you'd keep them somewhere close to you
Or maybe they'd just get mixed in with the cigarette butts you flick onto the ground.
And I'd get walked on

        And kicked around.

                And the truth is, I wouldn't even mind.

Because just through that, I would somehow be near you.

The Ghost

. . .

> I know you failed our happy ending
>
> And now you try to block me out of your life
>
> But every time you do something
>
> To try to show me that you don't care
>
> Anymore
>
> Only proves that you still do
>
> Like how you're reading this right now...

> Don't worry though
> Ghosts don't scare me

> And neither do you.

Your Biggest Regret

. . .

You'll miss me someday

You'll need me some time

Yet you do nothing to change this

So if you won't let me love you

Or be the love of your life

I'll be your biggest loss

Your biggest regret

Instead.

Strangers?

...

They say you can never take back time given

You can never get back the investments you made

Into another human's life

Like they did into yours

Yet part of me wishes I could forget you

Because maybe that'd be easier than moving on

But damn it, at the same time I wish

We could just go back to how it was

And now I'm laying here wondering

How do I now become strangers

With someone who has seen my soul?

I Hope You Miss Me

. . .

Most people would say "I hope you will always love me."

Some people might say "I hope I cross your mind often."

But I will say "I hope you miss me, darling."

For, in missing someone, you will consistently think of them.

You will always be reminded of the wonderful memories you share with them.
Of the times you loved them.

And those memories will always be present in your mind, not past.

Even if you hate me now, you will miss the times you loved me.

And the times that I loved you.

And only then, I feel, will you truly realize how deeply you cared for me.

And I for you.

So, my darling, I hope you miss me.

                         And most of all, know that I miss you too.

I Wonder, You Wonder

. . .

I hope some day you'll find something that used to belong to me
Something that I gave you as a keepsake
To remember me by

And I guess it worked
Because there you are
Looking at it, holding it
Thinking of me

And I hope you wonder if I still drive those same roads we used to
Or if I still murmur in my sleep

Maybe you'll even wonder if I still have that shirt
The one you loved to see me wear

Maybe you'll wonder if that song we used to call "ours"
Still makes me think of you every time it comes on the radio

But even more importantly than that,
I wonder
If you'll ever wonder
If I still wonder about you

And what used to be

What could have been
Us.

Looking Back Now

. . .

Looking back now, writing about him helped me heal.
It was part of the process of letting go of him, us, and what we had been.

Looking back now, I realize that I made him sound like such a special person. Someone who rocked my world but then left me empty and bruised. He didn't mean to, of course. I don't think any lover intentionally wants to hurt their other half. But I was fire and he was water and the two just don't mix.

Looking back now, I see that. And it really is okay. We have our share of beautiful memories. We have our brilliant display of lover's firework moments.

But it couldn't last.

Looking back now, maybe a part of us knew that at the time, but didn't want to admit it because giving life to such a thought was fearful.

We were a perfect match, and maybe that's why we burnt each other out.

We ended in a shadowy haze, because after all, does water know how to make a fire sizzle or how much it takes to put out the flame?

Last Chance To Say This

. . .

Why would I want anyone else back in my life when I have you? Every damn day, I would ask myself how I deserved someone like you. But apparently I didn't.

I wasn't meant to.

But for the time I did get to call you mine... I am so so thankful. Because you're a treasure.
You are an idiot. And one of the most difficult people I know, but your heart, your soul is so beautiful and kind and you care so much for so many people.

That's why I fell in love with you.

      That's why I love you.

No you're not perfect. But I'm not either.
And we've always accepted each other as such - or challenged each other to be better. *I hope* you'll always remember that part of me. You are such a treasure. Don't ever settle for someone who treats you as less than that. And this may be the last time I ever get to say this to you, so I will:

I love you.

And *I hope* that you'll always love the memories we made together.

I hope that when you sing along to "Body Like A Back Road" or "Despacito", you think of me.

I hope you think of me every time you see a star, stand in the rain, or watch the sky illuminate with fireworks.

I loved every part of you with every part of me.
Your name, your touch, or just your voice would make me revel in joy because I could say that you were mine.
That made me love life every day.

And I loved you with every single fiber of my being.

It Was Just a Breeze

. . .

Yes, we all experience getting over someone at different times, different paces, different everything. But there comes a point when you'll just have to discontinue.

Discontinue wishing they'd call you.

Discontinue typing out texts to send them but saving them to your notes instead.

Discontinue listening to old voicemails.

Discontinue making excuses.

Discontinue trying to justify their actions.

Discontinue going back to the person that you know is wrong for you.

It's hard. I know it's hard. It's excruciatingly painful sometimes.

There are 7 billion people in this world, though.
There are guys like him, there are girls like her.
But better.
Try imagining that for a second. Pretty crazy, huh? Because at one point of your life, you thought they were as good as it gets.
Well, they proved you wrong.
And now you're hurt.
You'll find someone else.
But first, you need to stop holding on to something that's not there anymore. You need to stop wishing that things could go back to the way they were when you were first in love, because that's like trying to grasp the air.
It's impossible.

It was a breeze that passed through your life, ruffled your hair and left it looking different, yes, but it didn't stick around to fix your wavy locks the way they were before.

I Promise, Your Heart Isn't Broken

. . .

"Heartbroken" is the term so often used to describe someone who has loved and lost.

You think that this pain will never cease. That it will just be something you get used to after an adequate amount of time has passed. It's not what you pictured life to be like a while ago, but hey, does anyone get the life they dreamed of?
And now you're afraid that this is all you'll ever know. How you loved, and how you lost, and how this writhing pain in your broken heart is just 'how life goes'.

You look back at the mass destruction of what used to be the love of your life. A love so passionate and strong that a wildfire couldn't burn it out. Or so you thought. But now it all lays in ruins around you and you think to yourself, "We must not have been that strong after all."

Right now, you may be reading this with puffy red eyes from crying yourself to sleep last night. Or you may have a stern, set look on your face because fine, it's over, you're moving on. But everyone feels some degree of pain after a heart wrenching end to a love. And nothing like it will ever happen to you again.

But hey, I have news for you. Love is not a restricted feeling. Love is not something you get a one time shot at and if you fail, oops you're done, disqualified, no more chances.

No. Love is a part of life. Love is a passion. A livelihood to any human soul. We were created with hearts, and the desire to love and be loved. It cannot be created again. It's already instilled in us. And it can't be destroyed. It can only be changed.

When someone has been "heart broken", they sometimes say something along the lines of "I will never love again". Oh but dear heart, you will. I promise you will. It will never be exactly the way it was before. Because how can you love two different people in the same exact way and form? You can't.

Your first love will always have a place in your heart. It was a special, life-changing kind of love. Something you had never felt before.
Loving a second time doesn't decrease or dismiss the first love you had.

Yes, everything you had was real. Yes, everything seemed perfect. But no, your heart isn't broken.

    And yes, you can love again.

    Someday, some time.

A time when you won't be able to stop it. It will just be. It will just happen, quite possibly contrary to your heart's demands.

And when it does, oh I hope you embrace it. I hope you find healing from your first heart crush - by knowing that it was a beautiful thing while it lasted, and it was true and it was real.

And now it's time to feel again.

And give that natural drive a second chance.

Never Stop Hoping

. . .

I was thinking today. (Not a rare occurrence, I assure you.)
But today, I was specifically thinking about how sad it is to know that after your first love, you will never be the same again.

You will never view love the same way.

You will never feel for someone the same way.

Because before your first love, your heart existed without being hurt. You were like a child, young and innocent, enjoying life for all it was worth. You didn't know the meaning of the word "pain". Everything was perfect in your eyes.

Until the day you were hurt.

And then, it was like a child seeing death for the first time.

You'll never view life the same way because you have seen the bad things that can happen, and how people can hurt others.
And after your first love, nothing will be the same because you know what love is, and you know that to love means to allow yourself to be hurt.

Crazy, isn't it?

You also learn something else after your first love, your first heart break, your first encounter with the painful side of loving someone.

You learn that no matter what happens, or how bad it seems, life does go on.

And it takes a day at a time to cry, to love yourself, to move on. And it takes even more time to allow yourself to begin to hope again.

And you need to allow yourself to hope.

Because without it, this world would be a much darker place.

You can't always live in fear and hopelessness that you're going to keep getting hurt. I'm not saying that you won't ever experience pain again. I wish I could promise you that we all feel it just once and then the rest of our lives are perfect.

But that's not the truth.

The truth is that hope is greater than fear.

And hope is the little candlelight against the vast darkness of unknown that will guide you to whatever and whoever God has in store for you.

Most of all, remember that you aren't alone in this struggle. Many people have been hurt. In fact, I can safely say, almost everyone has. Pain is a part of the process of life. It always will be on this earth.

But just because it's something you feel, doesn't mean it's something you have to be.

One of the greatest beauties in this world is seeing someone have the strength to rise after being beaten down,
to find the beauty in the ashes,
the courage to move on,
to start fresh.

Be that person.

And don't let a lost love define your future. Hope for an even better second love.

Or third.

Or fourth.

Just never stop hoping.

Dance With the Shadow

. . .

It's okay to think back on those memories
Just don't let the darkness of the past creep up on you
And envelop you
You, like everyone, will have good memories
And bad memories
Of the past
Their shadows will dance before your eyes at the most unexpected moments
You'll see something
Hear a song
Smell a scent
Walk into a building
And be flooded with the memories of a time
Not too long ago
When you were there
With that specific someone
And you won't be able to reach for their hand anymore
You won't be able to hug them
Or kiss their lips
But you'll only have the dark shadow of their ghost
And you can dance with it
But only for a moment
Because they aren't the reality anymore
The reality is that you did the right thing
For yourself
So dance with the shadow
But don't let it pull you back in

It's a memory

    Nothing more.

        Let it play out.

            And let it fade away

II. Lluvia

"Warm me like the sunlight and soothe me like the rain. Burn me with passion and steal away the pain."
- Tyler Knott Gregson

You Were My New Year

. . .

As I was recounting the past year, I realized that all the memories I held closest to my heart were ones that contained *you*. Your words, your smile, your touch.
We were inseparable.
      A unique bond.
And even though you have slowly faded from my life
There is one thing that will never change:

      You were my new year.

When we first became acquainted with the others' existence, it was as if two sparks met and started a flame. Together. And that flame burned long into the year.

Everywhere I turn, every thing I touch, every thing I wear, every song I listen to...
Everything holds a memory.
I can still hear you.
And see
and feel you.
I can still taste your mouth on my lips.

It hasn't faded. Even after a year. I still feel the whole zoo trampling in my stomach when I see your face or hear your name. Not just butterflies. Because you were more wild and mesmerizing than to make me feel just butterflies.
You were a raging ocean of magical waves, a sky full of starlit diamonds.
And when you looked at me, nothing else in the world mattered. Absolutely nothing.
I was content in just watching the way you held my gaze and the way you looked at me and knowing, with absolute certainty, that you loved me and I loved you. And that was enough.

      You were my new year.

And you were the best one I could have asked for.

The Madness

. . .

Being in love is madness.

It erupts - a **volcano** - then subsides.

But when this happens, there is a decision to make -
You have to work out whether your roots are so entwined together with another that it is inconceivable that you should ever part.

This is what love is.

Love itself is what is left over when being in love has burned away.

                        And this is both an art and a fortunate accident.

Don't Tell Me I Don't Know What Love Is

. . .

One thing I hate is when people say "You don't know what love is"...in comparison to their own personal experiences.

Every love is different.
It's not your place to tell someone that what they feel (or felt) isn't real.

When I have children, and they come to tell me that "Mama, I love this girl" or "Mama, I love this boy", I won't discourage them. I won't say "You can't love them. You don't know what real love is." Or "That's not real love, sweetheart, because it's not the kind of love Daddy and I share."
No.
If they believe that they love someone, I will let them love that person. As fully and as passionately as their little hearts know how to. Because there's something about that little love that made them label it "love", and who am I to say otherwise?

Love is quite possibly the most amazing, intense, crazy feeling you will ever know. It changes you. It takes you on an adventure. It makes you fly. How does a little child know what that's like? They may not understand it completely, but something about how they feel for someone makes their natural instinct kick in and say "What you're feeling right now is love."

How beautiful is that?

I think people compare others to themselves much too often. In all different situations in life. Not just love. And I think it's unfair to the whole human race that we are so quick to judge based on our own experiences.
Nothing happens the same way twice.
Nothing happens to two individuals the same exact way.
Give grace.
Listen with humility.

And above all, encourage the positive energy, the positive love, and the beautiful things in life.

Rest Stop Thoughts

. . .

I remember a time when I had given up

A time when I decided to pull over in a rest area on the highway of love
And take a nap

I was done with feeling

I was done with trying

I was done with being the misunderstood hopeless romantic I had come to be known as

I wore the title well
Until love had hurt me one too many times

Isn't that the funny thing about love though?
No matter how often it leads us down a path of illusion, we always seem to want more
But you, my darling, happened upon me like an early morning mist on the side of a hilltop
Something elegant and mysterious
And you made me curious
You piqued my interest
And above all, you made this callous heart feel something more than just a prick of a cold needle
You made it feel something warm
You made it feel something wonderful
You even made it stop beating for half a second every time your smile lit up my world
And my beautiful love, maybe I won't give up this time.
Would you like that?
Because I would.
I'll try again for you, if you'll let me
And I believe it would be one of the best decisions I've ever made.
Just don't leave my side, okay?
I can't do this without you.

Sometimes

. . .

Sometimes I wonder what it would be like if we had never met.
I wonder how different life would be...

Sometimes I wonder if you wonder the same things.

Maybe you would've met *some* other girl;
Made *some* other plans;
Fallen in love *some* other way.

Life might've been easier -
Or harder -
Or similar; yet not the same.

Sometimes I wonder if I had made different choices,
If we would've met under different circumstances...

Would we have started talking the way we had?
Would we have felt the same from the start?

All these things I wonder about *sometimes*

But I never wish them

Because wishing them would mean wishing you away.

I know for a fact
That I could never live any other way.

My wish is to never have to know what living without you would be like.

Sorry [not sorry] To Break It To You

. . .

True love isn't a perfect picture.

True love is a grueling army crawl through emotional barbed wire fences.

You are deciding to be romantically involved with a person who might very well break your heart. Or you break theirs.
Love and relationships should never be approached with the mentality that it will be full of candlelit dinners, long walks, cuddles, hugs and kisses. You need to be aware, you need to be cautious. Those romantic moments may come, but they are nothing to base a lifelong decision on.

This is the real world.

I know a lot of sheltered kids who, honestly, scare me at the thought of them being in a relationship one day. Many of them are taught that "God has the perfect one planned for you" and "He'll let you two meet at the perfect time", etc. Now don't get me wrong. I believe those two sentences to be incredibly and 100% true. But God also sends trials, tests, and difficulties our way. And your first boyfriend, your first girlfriend isn't always going to be "the one".

The truth of the matter is...
You may not be his first. You may not be her first. He may have cared for another girl before you. She may have kissed another guy before you. He's not perfect, but you aren't either. You're not the only girl he's ever made laugh or had that butterfly affect on.

So what are you going to do?

You're going to try and be the best you can be for them. Not because you're living *for* them, but because they make you happy, you make them happy and you want them to be a permanent part of your life. You're going to give them all you can. And you know what, sweetheart? You're giving him your heart. You're giving her your heart. A heart that they can break. And you have the power to break theirs too.

Love is about being selfless. It's about learning to care for them and even amidst trying your very hardest to treat them the ultimate best way they want to be treated, you might hurt them. And they might hurt you.
Don't take moments for granted. Smile when they make you happy. And miss them when they're not around.

So even though you're not their first, make yourself the most memorable.

And hopefully, the last.

Do not fall in love with only a body or a face.
And do not fall in love with the idea of love - for this is a dangerous place to be.
You need to fall in love even during the pain and the hardships and the cruel moments, because those are the moments of testing.

The moments of trusting that your love will overcome.

Trusting that love never does fail.

And trusting that the man or woman you love is the one who will forever be the one.

Love is a choice.

And it's tough, but it's possible

Just remember to fall in love with the choice that you will make to love and keep on loving one person.

You Are Merely The Wind

. . .

There comes a time when you realize something about yourself. And the way you feel for another.

It's that longing to always be with them.

Beside them.

Watching.

Touching.

The desire to be the cup of tea touching their lips in the morning, the bed they're resting on, the blanket they're cuddling with, the sunlight bathing their face with warm caresses.

You want to be the source of joy that brings those lips to curl in that beautiful smile, the light in their eyes, the gasp of breath from their lungs.

And with those desires, you pledge to do whatever it takes to win those as your trophies, as the target.

And you will accomplish it by reminding yourself that they are the arrow.

You are merely the wind.

My Reason

. . .

There's a reason why I woke up so early
There's a reason why I can't fall asleep
There's a reason why I'm thinking of you

And I wish that reason was in bed right beside me.

You

. . .

My fingers were twisting together like an old tree's roots, knotted and painful like the past I was explaining to you

You looked at me, your eyes full of patience as I stumbled over the words that were so hard to say

I told you of the times that hurt me deepest

I explained to you the reasons why I act the way I do sometimes

I relayed the moments of pure joy, pure sadness, pure ecstasy

And before I knew it, I let you into a room of my heart that I had never let anyone else in before
So quickly, so easily
I was able to bare my soul to you.

And you listened.

You laid there, propping yourself up
Looking down on my face
Your other arm resting gently on my stomach, your hand closed around my side
You watched as tears spilled gently from my eyes, onto the pillow beneath my head

And I described myself to you -

I told you that some days, I will forget how it is that I came to be with someone like you, and you might have to remind me why you love me

Some afternoons, I will stumble in the way I treat you, or block you out because I'm afraid you'll hurt me like others have before you, but I know that's not fair to you because you're nothing like them. (Please be patient with me when that happens. Just remind me that you're *you* and not *them*.)

And some nights I will be sunken in deep silence and you won't know how to pull me out of that forest of thoughts that fill my head.

Sometimes I need to feel the sadness in order to let it go

And sometimes, I'll share it with you -
Not for you to try to make me happy again but simply because I don't want to feel it alone

And when that sob began to rise in my chest, you gently laid a finger over my lips and said:
"Hey, I still love you. I always will."

And in that moment I knew the only thing that would be able to drag me out of the entanglement of memories is that voice

That touch

That *you*.

You Are My Perfect

. . .

I know perfection doesn't exist

But you exist

And in my eyes, that's much better

Because I'd rather have you - *a beautiful mess*

Than a perfect soul who I can't relate to.

If Our Eyes Could Tell Stories

. . .

If our eyes could speak -

What would they say?

Would they tell of the wonders seen;

Constellations above, the deep ocean beneath?

                                                Would they twinkle with mischief

                                                        As they blinked smiles away?

                                                            Would they close softly

                                                Afraid of what they would say?

If my eyes could speak...

They would say

"I have seen great beauties

But none as great as thee."

On the Wing of Tranquility

. . .

He and I went down to the water

And walked along it before finding a spot to pause and watch the sunset

To gaze over the small waves

I suddenly had this intensely scary feeling

I felt free

Happy.

It was scary because I felt it

Only because he was standing next to me

We weren't touching

We weren't speaking

Just standing. Still. Together.

And I felt like I was flying.

The Type Of Alcohol She Is

. . .

She's a tall glass of the strongest wine that will get you love drunk, while everyone else seems to be favoring the cheap beer that leaves them hungover.
And when the sun comes out, she'll be next to you in bed, while everyone else will be reeling with headaches on the floor.

I Doubt You'll Ever Read This

. . .

So many things remind me of you
Driving down certain roads
Listening to certain songs
The feel of a super fuzzy blanket
Or the smell of cigarette smoke
I still race other cars on the highway
The way you taught me
Even though the speed limit lowers around that one curve
I can't use that certain emoji without smiling a little too
I bought a black bandana to match with you
I don't know if you even realized I posted that picture on Snapchat for you to see it
Speaking of Snapchat, we never took a picture together
I don't think I'll ever forgive myself for that
Whenever I come across something relating to zodiacs, I always look at Scorpio
And I'll never forget that you helped me scratch off a couple things on my bucket list
Your hugs always felt warm
And I loved the way you grinned whenever we argued about who was taller
I swear I still am
Remember that wolf picture you sent me one time?
Or the bracelet you bought for me?
I still have it, of course
But the thread is coming apart and I'm afraid to wear it because it could come undone completely
I still have that note on my phone of your phrases
I don't think you'll ever read my little book
But it's nice to say all of this
Even if it's just for the sake of getting it out of my heart and brain
And onto a piece of paper
Oh and hey, just so you know,
Even though I never told you
I like the sound of your name.

Cigarettes

. . .

I hated the smell of cigarettes
But then I met you

And we were each other's winter fling

Most people have summer flings, right?

But we're unique

We're different

You once told me that you're like the devil

And I'm an angel

Such a strange and incompatible combination

I hate the smell of cigarettes
Until I tasted it on your lips

It made them tingle

Or maybe it was just the fact that you kissed me so well

You told me that you taught me how to kiss

But you didn't

And I know you know that

I hated the smell of cigarettes
Until I met you

And now, I'm jealous

Of any cigarette that you play with between your lips.

Our Story

. . .

I look at you and wonder

"Why did you ever pick me?"

Out of all the people in the world

You chose to be mine

You don't notice how I study you

Your every feature

Memorizing every line of your face

And damn, I think you're fascinating

I don't know why you love me like you do

You still haven't told me

But one thing I promise you, sweetheart

If you'll be my forever

I'll be your always

And I think our love will be spoken of for years to come

Of how two imperfect people

Were perfect for each other

Not because of the way they lived

But because of how they loved.

A Hundred More

. . .

There are so many little things about you that I love.

So many ways you move, words you say that I have memorized because they're my favorite things about you.

It's not the good job, the nice car, the good fashion sense.

It's the way you say my name, the way you reach for my hand, the way you smile when you see me from across the room.

But most of all, the way you make me feel.

Like you care.

As if I'm something special.

You told me once that time stops still for beauty and that the universe catches its breath for me.

It's not like me to fall, but I've fallen for you.

In more ways than one.

And every day I see you, I find a hundred more little reasons to love you.

In A Perfect World

. . .

If I had been the writer of our story, I would've planned our meeting differently.

I would have planned it for a different time in my life.

A time when I wasn't so skeptical and quick to be a pessimist.

I would have planned it for a time when I was more hopeful, not so scared to meet someone and develop feelings so quickly.

For you.

In a perfect world, the first person you love is your forever love, the one who will never leave, the one love you will always have in your life till the end of time.

In a perfect world, your first encounter with love is your best, your favorite, and your only.

In a perfect world, love would always be a good thing, not something you would ever doubt, not something that causes you to be fearful.

But as many of us know - you included, I think - is that love happens at the most unexpected times. You don't even realize what's happening until after the fact.
Until after you've fallen for someone who, a week, a month or a year ago, was a complete stranger.
And now they've become the most important, significant, special person in your life.

That's you in mine.

Do you know how often I've wished I could meet someone like you?
And how often the thought has crossed my mind that I might never have that wish granted to me?
All those 11:11 wishes were about you.
Before I even knew you existed.

You were the one my subconscious only dreamed of.

And I think all that wishing and hoping and praying somehow brought you to life.

Or at least I'd like to think it had some sort of effect on your wonderful existence.

You are wonderful, you know that?

It's 1:09am as I sit and write this.

Your face keeps coming to mind.

I keep replaying some of my favorite memories with you over and over in my brain and I smile to myself. Not just because I love those memories, but because I'm so happy that even after not very much time has passed since that day you entered my life and exploded it with color, we have already made so many memories.

And I'm in love with them.

In fact, I'm in love with you.

And I'm so lucky to love you.

> Thank you for letting me be the one to love you.

Loving Someone Is a Privilege

. . .

Loving someone is a privilege.

It's a rare occurrence when someone trusts you with their heart and gives you the power to either bless or break it.
But everyone loves differently, and needs to be loved differently. And because love is selfless, it's important to love them the way they need to be loved.

While your significant other may need words of affirmation, but you are more of a physical touch person, learn to love them through words that they need to hear.

Or if you feel loved through acts of service, but your partner feels love most through gifts, then they need to learn how to help you with projects and not expect you to feel love from them through buying you gifts that they would like.

Relationships take time and effort. You should never change who you are for someone else, unless it's in a healthy way. And learning how to live and love to make your partner happy and feel loved can be a rough road sometimes.

Relationships aren't easy. It's about two imperfect people choosing each other above anyone else they know or will meet and continuing to choose that person through the good, the bad and the ugly.

Learn about your significant other.

Learn how to love them because after all, they're giving you that special honor to care for them and their heart.

They don't need you to survive this life.
They're choosing to let you be a part of it.

Don't take that for granted.

And don't let them regret their choice.

You're Not The Only Guy Who Will Love Her Well

. . .

To every guy with a girlfriend...

Don't think for one second that you're the only guy who will treat her this well. Cuz I can promise you that you aren't. There are hundreds of thousands of men out there who know how to treat a woman like a queen. You're not some magical exception.

Does her very essence cause chills down your spine?
Do you quake at the sound of her voice?
Or tremble at her touch?
Good.
For her love should be something you fear with high regard. It is not something she gives lightly. She is allowing you to be in her life. She is choosing you.
The chaotic storm that resides in her brain, the raging seas in her veins, the ever constant flutter of her heart, amidst it all, she decides to be with you.
Her soul is a strange and beautiful one.
She can be fierce, yet gentle.
Strong, yet humble.
She can make you feels things and take you places you have never been before.
And she will love you through it if you treat her well.
Learn from her.
Cherish her.
Love her tenderly.
Love her the way she wants to be loved, not the way you think is best.
She is so much more than a pretty face and a hot body.
She is a beautiful human.
She is a fiery soul, intent on living life to its fullest.
And she doesn't have to do it with you.
She'll do it with your help or without your restriction.
What you should focus on is being the guy who treats her so well that she decides no other guy is worth being with and will stay with you.

And don't you dare take her for granted.

To My Future Husband, Please Don't Feel Guilty

. . .

My dearest love,

So often I think this world tells us to hide our past, and to cower with shame at little mistakes or certain events that took place.

But I want you to know that you must never feel guilty about telling me anything.

I want to know every little thing about you, every secret, every wish, every regret.

I want you to be able to come to me and tell me about the worst thing you think you've ever done but be assured that my affection for you won't change.

I want to know your story.

I want to know about your first love, about the love you found and lost.

I want to know how she hurt you.

I want to know what went wrong.

Please tell me what she did to make you shy or how she made you cry.

Tell me about your first kiss, your first date, your first dreams, your first fears.

Point out every scar that you have from falling and fighting your way to me.

Tell me the stories behind each mark on your skin, every cut in your heart.

Let me kiss your wounded hands that are sore and calloused from picking up the pieces of your heart that she left.

Please don't hide anything from me.

For I, likewise, will tell you of my journey.
And while it may hurt others to hear of their lover's firsts, to me, it just shows that you have cared, that you can feel, that your heart is soft and loving.

I don't hate your past or anyone from it. All I care about is you.

Here and now.
With me.

We've all been broken at some point of our lives. The pain we felt made an eruption in our hearts.

But it doesn't change the fact that we are two human souls, yearning for the surface to break of the water we are under.

And to find each other.

And believe me that someday, when I do find you, I will strive to treat you the way you need and desire to be treated.

I will yearn with every fiber in my being to love you the way you want and deserve to be loved.

And I think that's when we'll both find that balance of love and happiness that we thought we'd found long ago with someone else...

But couldn't experience it to the fullest until we had found each other.

Tribute To Love

. . .

When you showed me your ring, the diamond as bright as the smile on your face, my heart was so happy for you, my friend. To think that you finally reached the day that you'd been waiting for and praying about...and now, it was finally here.

When you told me of the look on her face, while you asked the special question that you'd been dying to ask, your eyes radiated with love as you described the beauty that you see in the woman of your dreams.

Little by little, one by one, I have seen God work mightily through your lives. Sometimes in small detail perhaps, but nonetheless, powerful. Every drop, every wave, every crash and cloud and clap of thunder through the rain, He composed a song and a dance only for you and yours. Until they collided into one, and you can't dance a note more unless you dance it together.

But along the way, somehow, He had designed a passionate love to knit your hearts together, so that when you wed, it was as perfect as two puzzle pieces - so totally different but so perfectly designed for each other. A passionate love that grew, and will continue to grow, over time.

When your heart finds its match, it is as if a volcano will erupt unless the two be joined.
And when they do, you must decide.
Each for yourself:

Shall you release all that you had known of before, everything you held dear, and cling with all your might to the one now before you?

Will nothing ever stop you from parting ways?

Is this love strong enough to withstand the most ferocious flame, the most threatening blizzard, the longest fall into sorrow?

People don't believe in true love anymore. What with the way today's world has painted a picture of it as a fairytale sort of wispy love and a happy ending that can only transpire when the two lovestruck individuals throw themselves into each other's arms, with no thought to the future.

But wait. Is this what being in love really is?

Being in love has many moments of feelings, such as losing one's breath when your beloved says your name, or entwining your fingers with the one who you know will absolutely never let you go, or to lie awake at night knowing that someone somewhere is thinking of you - specifically of you.

I have seen this many times. And what I have seen with my own eyes far outweighs any love story that was ever written by any mere man.

But what of these people who make up silly stories of what "being in love" is?

Well, I believe they say such things because they don't understand something. They don't understand that amidst the troubling hardships and thorns of life, love is hidden throughout in a myriad of different details.
It may subside, for love is a temporary madness. There will come a time when your kisses may not be as passionate.
One of you may forget a special occasion or anniversary.
One of you will unintentionally insult the other. And perhaps there will be raised voices during an argument. These are all just ruts in the road.

Do you not know, though, that anything can withstand time only by enduring the messy bits? Life is the messy bits. And oh what a beautiful life to live and to share with the one who has promised to love you, body and soul, through it all.

Stay with him, not for all the things he has done right, but for the choice that you made: to love and cherish him all the days of your life.

Choose not to leave her for the one thing she did wrong, but to stay with her for all the things she had done right.

Society says "oh but if such and such happens, he doesn't love you anymore" or "if she says this or that, the love she promised you was a lie."

So I challenge you -

When those rough waves come, when the ship of your marriage is being tossed to and fro, hold tight to each other with one hand, and hold on for life with the other. To the main mast of your ship. The pillar of strength. The only One who can see you through any storm.

Afterall, He is the Designer of all things. Even such a story as slaying His own Son so that you might have a perfect example of what true love is.

This is true love.

True love is breaking yourself in half so that you can be joined with another half to become one.

There will be constant breaks, yes, constant bendings, and fittings, and stretchings. And with these comes pain, for this is a union of two hearts, two souls, two personalities.

But true love is what stands when everything else has fallen.

True love is what is left when all around you has burned away.

Defy what society calls love and stand for what they call impossible.

Success is the greatest revenge. Avenge the dying legacy of what true love really is.

And with every passing day you live as one heart bound to another, I pray that the little spark which started this dazzling flame, will only continue to be fed
And that soon, the world will stop and gaze in astonishment at something they deemed impossible.

III. Petrichor

"Your body is a museum of natural disasters. Can you grasp how stunning that is?"
- Rupi Kaur

Welcome

. . .

I'll give you a tour of my soul

But please leave your shoes at the door

I don't need the dust from your life

Mixing in with mine

For I cannot handle my own decisions sometimes

And much less can I afford to give away the energy and strength it takes

To keep myself alive.

Hey Fear

. . .

Hey Fear,

I have news for you.

You're not welcome here anymore.

I have constantly cowered at your accusing, pointing finger, telling me that I'm not worth it, not able to succeed, and that I will never amount to anything.

I have denied opportunities, turned away from exciting potential, and constantly talked negatively to myself. I put into words all the thoughts you put into my head.

You have been a torment, a torture, a constant pang of guilt and misery. You have lied to me and chained me and held me back from doing things I should have done.

But I'm done now. I don't want to have you in my life anymore. You have no power over me.

I reach out and break your bony finger.

I will not fear!

Although I may feel your disgusting presence, I will not give in to your demands.
I have a new companion - a Friend, not a tormentor.

You can try to bring me down, to hurt me, to try to regain status in my life, but greater is He who is in me than you who are of the world.

So hey fear,

You're not welcome here.

Music is in My Blood

. . .

Do you ever get that feeling?
Late at night, lying in bed
You're the only one awake.
And your mind begins to wander
To journey
Skipping from star to star in the randomness of your sky thoughts.
It's as if a whole universe is inside of just you.
Grievous things are happening on one planet, while the other is full of laughter and happiness.

But amidst the chaos of two or three or four completely different emotions, lies one art that combines them all.

The blood streaming through your very being is made of up notes...

Music.

A form of communication.
One of the most powerful known to mankind. Through it, you can say many things. Or by it, you can say few words that communicate myriads of thoughts and feelings that could not otherwise have been spoken. It is a source of comfort, of pain, of truth, of self-confidence, of love, of worship.

A passion.
Something you are either born with or must come to appreciate and love. It is, or becomes, part of who you are. Part of why you live. Part of how you survive. Everyone's ears and hearts are tuned differently. But in all of us, is the underlying commonness we share when our hearts - not our ears - listen to the music.

A release.
Music may not be a physical form of art, but if, and when, it symbolizes exactly what you're thinking or feeling, it strikes a chord in your that may be painful, but oh so perfect.

A description.
Music can do what no words can. With it, you can express your thoughts, your feelings; it can bring back memories, or create new ones. The best music is the kind that you can listen to while standing completely still, but feel like you're soaring through the air. When words seem insufficient to explain and describe your thoughts, music can make those words and you say "Here, listen to this. For right now, I cannot speak."

A way of survival.
Only true musicians will understand when I say that music is another way of breathing. It's not just a part of life. It's a part of my being, of who I am. I don't just listen to music. I don't just play music. I feel it. I let it coarse through my veins, I let it seep into my pores, I let every note strum on my heartstrings until it is not the speakers echoing the sound but my very soul.

Whilst In Your Twenties

. . .

"Nothing will ruin your twenties more than thinking you should have your life together already."

This statement resonated so deeply with me.

The path to our destination is not always a straight one. It's a rather scenic route.
And what if it's not about which road we take, but what we embark on. Is it on our own judgement and the way we feel? Or the truth that our soul knows and can trust?

Life is amazing and awful all at the same time. And in between these climax moments is the routine, the everyday, the ordinary. But the truth is that each of these times has significance in your growth. If you were to fast forward ten years from now and choose to look back on these moments, you will see why they had to happen and for what purpose.

God says, "You're gonna be happy, but first, I'm gonna make you strong." Because without the painful times of maturing, you won't enjoy the good times as much.

I know people who graduated college at the age of 19.
I know people who were making a million dollar budget by the time they were 25.
I know people who are single and have children.
Or people who are married but waited 5-10 years before having children.
I know people who love each other but aren't together.
Or people who hate each other but are married. T
here are people waiting to love and who have so much love to offer.

You don't have to do anything just because you see others doing them or because someone tells you that it's what you should do.

I promise that the day you stop giving weight to people's opinions of what you "need to do" with your life, is the day you will feel free.

The point is, everything in life happens according to the time allotted us. It may not seem fair, but the beauty of trusting in a sovereign Creator is knowing that He has a purpose through it all. You may look at your friends and think "Oh they have their lives together", "They're so far ahead, and I'm so far behind", or "Why can't my life look more like theirs?"

Be patient.

You're right where you're supposed to be.

The best advice I've been given as a twenty-something year old is:

l e a r n

Ask questions
make mistakes
learn from them.

A wise man once said -
"Don't regret things.

Why?

Because you never lose in life.

You either win or you learn."

You Are A Work of Art

. . .

You can't tell me you're worthless

You can't convince me that you have nothing to offer

That there is no beauty within your self

How can you sit there and tell me that you're not amazing

When I can clearly see galaxies of stars in your eyes -

The spitfire determination in your heart?

I can see things blossom under your touch

Your gifts and talents could illuminate a room of a thousand people

Your body is made up of a million magnificent little cells

All coming together to form such a work of art

To make you

You are an unusual and unique piece of human flesh

Designed solely for the purpose of housing a soul -

A gorgeous and mesmerizing and awe-inspiring soul

A spirit of life and daring and true love

You are a work of art

Don't you dare try to persuade me otherwise.

Unbreakable

...

I love you for being so unbreakable

You have fought and conquered
You have fought and been defeated
But neither end results have wavered my admiration for you
Your heart
Your character
Both so strong
Yet so fragile

I love you for being so unbreakable

No matter the constant flurry of trials and pain
That life sends your way
You are steadfast
Resolved
A resolute rock, sturdy amidst the crashing waves

I love you for being so unbreakable

You are a true example for many to learn from
Your legacy will be written of in the sky, in the sand
An individual who is firm regardless of the times you've been beaten down
You always manage to stand back up
To move forward
To fight another day

I love you for being so unbreakable

And for encouraging me to do the same.

Made For Magnificence

. . .

Everywhere you look, the world subtly - and sometimes not so subtly - tells us that we are defined by others' opinions of us.

Our popularity is ranked by how many Facebook or Instagram likes we receive on a daily basis. And if we are well-liked, we'll have hundreds of followers on social medias.

The internet and magazines are constantly nagging us with ads on weight loss, skin care, hair product, and the latest beauty secrets.

Because of all these, we think we are made up of numbers - price tags, scale pounds, grades, likes on social medias.

But are we really?

Is this who you want to be known as? Is this the legacy you want to leave behind - someone who believed that something immortal could define who they were as an eternal soul? We allow things to have such a hold on our lives, on our hearts, when in reality, we're the ones who are in control of who and what defines us.

You know what I think?

I think we're made up of love, of memories, of pain. By the words we speak, the actions we follow through with.
What defines us is what happens in our lives, the moments we learn, the moments we feel, the moments we will never forget, not even in a million years.

We're made of late nights with friends, or random mini roadmaps, taking a sip of your favorite drink on a brisk autumn evening or a stifling summer's day, watching a sunset from a rooftop, buying a pair of jeans that fit just right, the art we love, warm blankets in a cold room, the way music makes us feel or that moment when you look into the eyes of someone you love and know without a doubt that they love you back.

We're defined by what we allow to define us.

We're lit on fire by flames that ignite many different blazes but we're all affected the same way.

This thing called life that we're trying to survive...
Why can't we all just realize that we're in this fight together?

Everyone has struggles, everyone is being told they're defined by numbers. But we need to rally together. We need to acknowledge the brainwashing of today's culture and say no to being put into a box and labeled as a certain someone, a certain thing.

Because we're more than that.

You are more than that.

Underneath all the layers of skin that clothes your body, you are a living and breathing soul that was intricately designed by the breath - not the fingers - of the Creator of the galaxies.

You are special because He says you are.

You are defined as who He says you are.

Your label is not one of a mere product of earth, but of a handmade piece of art that He carefully and masterfully designed to be so breathtakingly beautiful.

We are more than numbers. We are more than what they tell us we are.

We are magnificent.

Shoutout To You

. . .

Working in the coffee industry has been enlightening in the fact that I get to meet and interact with many different kinds of individuals.

It's also taught me something about life that I'm not sure I would have otherwise ever learned.

Since being a barista for over three years, one huge part of my job that I've come to realize is that a barista is almost like a therapist. We serve so many different people throughout a shift and by the end of the day, we have had so many stories told to us, so many hugs given, sometimes tears shed.

We're entrusted with narratives of car accidents, weddings, funerals, pets.
We meet the businessman needing a strong cup of coffee to start his day at the office.
Or the mom running errands before picking up her kids from school.
Or the groom on his way to get married.
Or the traveler, who is road tripping to this or that state.
Or the high schooler who just attended their best friend's funeral.

The reoccurring theme I see in the faces, the smiles, and the stories can be summed up in one word:

s u r v i v a l

We're all attempting to live this life, to get through it one day at a time.
We're all trying to survive.

And we all do it differently.

For example, I'm sitting here in bed, wearing an XXL men's hoodie, eating pizza, drinking pink moscato, and unwinding after a twelve and a half hour work day and not getting home till 1am.

That's how I'm choosing to live my tonight. That's how I'm deciding to survive.
And no, I didn't get everything accomplished today that I wish I had. And I may not finish my "to do" list tomorrow.

But you know what?
I'm going to try.

The sun will rise and I will try again.

And keeping trying.

    And keep surviving.

        And damn it, I hope you do too.

I hope you wake up tomorrow morning, eager for another day on this beautiful earth.

I hope you choose to make it even more beautiful.

I hope you stop and notice a little detail amidst your busyness and smile because you know God chose to do add a spark to your day.

And I hope you keep trying, keep surviving.

This is a shoutout to you.

There's never going to be enough time to do everything you want to do, but at least try, okay?

Try to make time for yourself.
Reward yourself for getting things done, for getting through the day without snapping.
Because that's a huge accomplishment in and of itself.

Keep it up.

You're doing great.

To the One Who Taught Me All I Know

. . .

It all started by choosing to give me life

You fed and cared for me long before my little body was born
And when the day came
To let me enter the world
You experienced stress and pain
Only for the end result to be my tiny self, enveloped in your arms
And you fed and cared for me there too

I grew and grew
You watched and protected

You were there when I took my first steps

You were there when I took my first fall

You were there when I said my first word

And comforted me every time I cried

You have been the only steadfast person I know

When I was little, your leg was what I reached for to keep my balance

When I was older, your arms were what held me up when I was broken

Throughout my years of life, you were my constant
The one I could go to for any emergency, great or small
Whether because I scraped my arm
Or when someone bruised my heart

You taught me what it means to forgive
You taught me the importance of being patient

You have always been my biggest fan
My greatest encourager
My ever loyal and relentless friend
But more than that, you have been *my mother*

Not just a parent, not just a protector
But the one human in all the world who I can always count on

The one I can call in the middle of the night
The one I can depend on to be there for me at my lowest
The one whose arms I long to have wrapped around me when there is no one else to hold me

Your commitment to our family

Your excellent love for my Dad

Your determination in your work

All of it is so honorable and worthy of recognition

More precious than jewels

And though you may be an imperfect human

You fear the One who made you

And for that, I praise you.

Shine Bright, You Crazy Diamond

. . .

I like to think that every living human has a bit of the "I want to save the world" mentality.

It's not very often that I find someone who shares that same passion with me, that same drive. To leave a mark on this world, albeit small.
I don't meet very many individuals like that.
But the ones I do meet, I crave to be around.
Because I think two is better than one. And three is better than none.

But there's another kind of thought process that I think we need to remind ourselves of.

And it is this:

No matter how much you want to save the world, you need to know that saving just one person is enough.
And if that person is you, it's okay.

I believe there is only One who can truly save you from all that is evil and corrupt in this world. And only one place where nothing will ever harm you again.
But what I'm saying is that while living in this world, you can't depend on others.
Yes, there are many people who will love you, care for you, but they're humans - just like you. And they will fail. They will fall short. They won't always be there for you. Don't let this make you mad. Don't let it harden you. Don't let the pain, that I guarantee you will experience in life, make you hate. Don't let bitterness steal your joy. Because at some point, you're going to have to stop.

Stop being angry.

Stop being sad.

Stop hurting yourself and learn instead that it's okay to be gentle.

It's okay to admit you need help.

You need to learn to embrace love and acceptance instead of being afraid of it.
You have to love yourself.

Learn to care for and respect your body.
Learn to show others you care for yourself and deserve to be treated as the beautiful human you are.

Don't waste time being unhappy.

Don't waste time trying to be like someone else.

Don't think that there's all to life - to be better than the next person.

Don't do this to yourself.

And don't let others tell you what to be.

You are you.

That's who you were created to be.
Explore that.
Find what that means.
Search after His design for you with all your heart and it will be made clear to you.
Maybe not today, or tomorrow, or next year. It might take your whole life. But what an adventure that will be!
Have goals and dream big, but don't focus on what can happen in a month or a year. Things can change in the blink of an eye.
Instead, you need to fix your attention on today, the next twenty-four hours, and do whatever you can in that amount of time to get closer to where you want to be tomorrow. Just a day at a time.

Discover your vision and your goals as early as possible. Find what you're passionate about and follow it. Become aware of what's important to you and show it to the world. Live life from the heart. Don't let magazines, billboards, television or the internet tell you what to do and who to be. You are your own person. You don't need to be validated by the world. Live for people, but not for their approval.

Shine your light. Because you're a beautiful diamond all on your own.

Me

. . .

I dream too much for how little I write.
I look for God in everything.
I look for beauty in the little things, memories in the small moments.
I find adventure wherever I can.
I stand in awe of things most people may overlook.
I tend to apologize too often for things I am not sorry I said.
And at the end of the day, my biggest regret is not doing more than I did.

Closing note from the author

. . .

Honestly, dear readers, the words don't always come easily.

You may have picked up this little book because you've read my other work, or perhaps the title caught your attention, or maybe a friend recommended it to you. You may think I'm a good writer. You may picture me in a romantic scene, thinking up whatever words you enjoy reading and typing them away without a care in the world.

But, I'll be real with you.

Sometimes, it's painstakingly hard. First of all, to sort through my thoughts; secondly, to know how to express them with words; and thirdly, to allow every eye to see them.

I asked myself almost every day, "Why do you write?"

I always answer the same thing, "Because I couldn't live without being able to."

I do it because I find freedom in this gift of an outlet.
I find freedom in expressing myself with passion and purpose through beautiful, beautiful words.

Language is such a **gift**. To have the ability to communicate to someone not just through facial expressions and hand movements but to actually speak and be understood is so wonderful.
To be able to write and have a reader halfway across the world grasp your meaning and fervor in being vulnerable and revealing your heart, soul and emotions...

Now that's a blessing.

I write because I can't imagine not being able to write something and send it out to somehow, magically find someone and touch their soul.
For the heart to resonate with something I wrote, and to maybe later find an email or comment from that someone saying, "Hey, what you said really encouraged me" or "Your words were an inspiration". Those little notes make it all worth it. Just to know one person (yes, even the haters <3) read something I scribbled at one o'clock in the morning means the world to me.

Because, honestly, you don't have to.

You didn't have to pick this book up today.
You didn't have to go check out the newest link to my blog that popped up in your email, on your dashboard or Facebook timeline.
You didn't have to read all the way until the end of this book.

But wow.

You did. You're here.

So thank you. From the depths of my heart, thank you.

A writer's daily battle may be figuring out what thought to write down first and how to word it well and if we did it right and oh what if it doesn't make sense, etc., etc...
but our greatest victory is knowing one - even just one beautiful human being - chose to read our work.

Then yes, we have done well. Our readers are our greatest reward.

And if you're still reading this, if you made it to the end, then I have done well.

www.ingramcontent.com/pod-product-compliance
Lightning Source LLC
Chambersburg PA
CBHW061338040426
42444CB00011B/2977